Bakeries

Level 8 – Purple

Helpful Hints for Reading at Home

The graphemes (written letters) and phonemes (units of sound) used throughout this series are aligned with Letters and Sounds. This offers a consistent approach to learning, whether reading at home or in the classroom.

HERE IS A LIST OF PHONEMES FOR THIS PHASE OF LEARNING. AN EXAMPLE OF THE PRONUNCIATION CAN BE FOUND IN BRACKETS.

Phase 5			
ay (day)	ou (out)	ie (tie)	ea (eat)
oy (boy)	ir (girl)	ue (blue)	aw (saw)
wh (when)	ph (photo)	ew (new)	oe (toe)
au (Paul)	a_e (make)	e_e (these)	i_e (like)
o_e (home)	u_e (rule, cube)		

Phase 5 Alternative Pronunciations of Graphemes			
a (hat, what)	e (bed, she)	i (fin, find)	o (hot, so, other)
u (but, unit)	c (cat, cent)	g (got, giant)	ow (cow, blow)
ie (tied, field)	ea (eat, bread)	er (farmer, herb)	ch (chin, school, chef)
y (yes, by, very)	ou (out, shoulder, could, you)		

HERE ARE SOME WORDS WHICH YOUR CHILD MAY FIND TRICKY.

Phase 5 Tricky Words			
oh	their	people	Mr
Mrs	looked	called	asked
could			

TOP TIPS FOR HELPING YOUR CHILD TO READ:

• Allow children time to break down unfamiliar words into units of sound and then encourage children to string these sounds together to create the word.

• Encourage your child to point out any focus phonics when they are used.

• Read through the book more than once to grow confidence.

• Ask simple questions about the text to assess understanding.

• Encourage children to use illustrations as prompts.

This book focuses on /ie/ and /ea/ and the alternative pronunciations of their graphemes. It is a Purple level 8 book band.

Which of these items do you think you might find in a bakery?

A baker is a person who makes bread, cakes, pastries and other baked goods. They may sell their goods to shops or display them in their own bakeries.

Bakers have to get up before most people so that they have time to set up before people come to get breakfast. They may wake up while it is still dark.

It is important for bakers to have good hygiene. They keep their hands, tools and worktops clean while they bake. They may wear aprons and tie their hair up, too.

Bakers must keep track of what is in each baked good so that people with allergies do not get ill. They use labels so that people know what is in them.

To get a perfect bake, bakers have to use exact amounts. They cannot just add random amounts of yeast or eggs. If they do, the baked goods will not come out right.

Mixing correctly is important, too. If bakers mix a batter for a long time instead of giving it a brief fold, they may end up with a flat cake.

While some baked goods can be made in a short amount of time, bread needs quite a while. Bakers have to wait for bread to rise before they bake it. This is called proofing.

To make bread rise, bakers add yeast to the mix. When the mix is set aside in a place that is not too cold, it will expand to fill the pot.

After it is proofed and shaped, bread goes on a tray and is baked. Bread expands as it bakes, so bakers make sure to spread out the lumps so that they do not stick when they rise.

Bakers can tell when bread is well-baked as it turns golden and gives off a pleasant smell. They let it cool on racks.

At some bakeries, you can get tier cakes. These are cakes that have a number of stacked layers. They may be decorated with lots of flowers and berries.

Think ahead to the next time you are going to bake. What will you make? You could make a pie, a pizza base, gingerbread cookies and more!

©2023 **BookLife Publishing Ltd.**
King's Lynn, Norfolk, PE30 4LS, UK

ISBN 978-1-80505-091-9

All rights reserved. Printed in China.
A catalogue record for this book is available from the British Library.

Bakeries
Written by Charis Mather
Designed by Lucy Otter

An Introduction to BookLife Readers...

Our Readers have been specifically created in line with the London Institute of Education's approach to book banding and are phonetically decodable and ordered to support each phase of the Letters and Sounds document.

Each book has been created to provide the best possible reading and learning experience. Our aim is to share our love of books with children, providing both emerging readers and prolific page-turners with beautiful books that are guaranteed to provoke interest and learning, regardless of ability.

BOOK BAND GRADED using the Institute of Education's approach to levelling.

PHONETICALLY DECODABLE supporting each phase of Letters and Sounds.

EXERCISES AND QUESTIONS to offer reinforcement and to ascertain comprehension.

CLEAR DESIGN to inspire and provoke engagement, providing the reader with clear visual representations of each non-fiction topic.

AUTHOR INSIGHT:
CHARIS MATHER

Charis Mather is a children's author at BookLife Publishing who has a love for reading and writing. Her studies in linguistics and experiences working with young readers have given her a knack for writing material that suits a range of ages and skill levels. Charis is passionate about producing books that emphasise the fun in reading and is convinced that no matter how much you already know, there is always something new to learn.

This book focuses on /ie/ and /ea/ and the alternative pronunciations of their graphemes. It is a Purple level 8 book band.

Image Credits Images are courtesy of Shutterstock.com. With thanks to Getty Images, Thinkstock Photo and iStockphoto. Cover – alexdndz, Krakenimages.com, MaraZe, Miller Inna. 3 – Valentin Valkov, Stepan Bormotov, Naruedom Yaempongsa, Olhastock, VictorH11, seksan wangjaisuk, SeDmi. 4–5 – Kues, Viktoriia Hnatiuk. 6–7 – Daisy Daisy, Tyler Olson. 8–9 – BongkarnGraphic, PeopleImages. com – Yuri A. 10–11 – casanisa, Natalya_Maisheva. 12–13 – Luciavonu, Maurizio Milanesio. 14–15 – Melnikov Sergey, Monkey Business Images.